Why Me?

A Time in My Life

ZAINORA POLK

PAGE PUBLISHING, INC.
Conneaut Lake, PA

First originally published by Page Publishing 2022

ISBN 978-1-6624-6898-8 (pbk)
ISBN 978-1-6624-6899-5 (digital)

Printed in the United States of America

To my favorite guys; my husband, Edward, and my son, Ethan. Edward, thank you for being nothing but supportive and encouraging throughout this entire process. I thank God daily for giving me such an understanding and caring husband. Thank you for all your support; you truly are my *rock*. I love you! To my baby boy, Ethan, you are the light of my life; thank you for teaching me how to be a better me. Mommy loves you.

Contents

Prologue

First Day of Dialysis

When my husband and I arrived at the clinic, my emotions were all over the place. I was not handling it well, not knowing what to expect, not knowing what I would see once I was in the "back." I was nervous and scared. I said to myself, *Lord, why am I here? I should not be on dialysis.*

As my husband and I sat in the lobby area, waiting for my name to be called to go to the back, I saw people come in and wait with me. I also saw a few patients came from their treatment in the back. Seeing those patients leaving, some looked tired and sleepy, and some were waiting on their transportation to return to pick them up. Again, I was questioning God, *Why me?*

The nurses called my name, and I went to the back while the receptionist instructed my husband on the time for him to return and pick me up. In the back, I sat in what looked like a recliner chair. I looked around at the different patients in the large room and looked at the machine that was there next to me. At that moment, I felt like I wanted to cry because I genuinely believed that this was all a dream. Something I prayed so hard against…I was now there. A deep sigh came over me, and I thought, *This is the new norm, so get used to it.*

Chapter 1

The Big Move
108 Days Married and in Route To California

Our day began at 5:00 a.m. I don't think I slept all night because I was so excited about leaving Tennessee and starting a new life in California for the next four years. My reason for being so excited was because it was a new life that Edward and I both got to share together. Edward and I were both on active duty in the US Navy, and we'd now been assigned to San Diego, California. We left Tennessee at 6:30 a.m. with a loaded SUV and a quick prayer for traveling grace and mercy, and we began our road trip.

We drove until the sun began to set and found a place to lay our heads for the night, only to rise the next morning and continue our journey.

We finally made it to San Diego, and boy, were we glad! When we arrived, the weather was great. It was seventy-five degrees and sunny in November. When we left Tennessee, it was about forty-five degrees, so to go from wearing a jacket to not wearing a jacket felt great. We spent the next three days in San Diego unpacking and trying to make our new place feel like home. Still excited about the new location, Edward and I finished unpacking early so we decided to go sightseeing.

It was vital to my husband and me that we found a church that we both liked. So on different Sunday mornings, we took time to attend fellowship in different churches. We visited one church, in particular, that was recommended to us and that was the best move we could've made. We knew as soon as we departed from the church that day that we would soon make it our church home. When we joined the church, we met some amazing people that we grew to adore. This church was filled with a lot of active duty and retired military, which made us feel comfortable. We knew it was a place that my husband and I could grow spiritually.

It was December 2008, and it was time for me to check into my new duty station. In doing so, I met a lot of sailors whom I would be working with for the next three years. Since I was on shore duty,

Edward was now stationed on a ship that would do a short deployment for training soon.

Six months we'd been married, and the time had come for Edward to go on a short deployment. We had not been separated for more than a few hours, so the deployment would take some getting used to. I felt this short deployment was harder on me than it was on him because we were in a new area, and I did not have any friends or family close to me. I really felt alone with Edward being away, but that was the time that my church family stepped in and showed me so much love while he was away. They took time for me and saw how I was while Edward was away and took me in as their family.

The time came for Edward to return home from the short deployment, and I was so excited to have him home. While he was home, we both took a few days off and decided to continue to explore San Diego. We had come to realize that we really liked the city.

Chapter 2

Living in Sunny California

A navy deployment typically consists of two or more ships traveling together to and from a specific region and/or an area. The deployment is usually for one particular mission and/or training for all the sailors aboard the ship.

With my husband being stationed on a ship in San Diego, he could be scheduled to deploy at any time and that time had come for him to leave with his ship for a six-month deployment. While my husband was away, I was working and decided to go back to school to obtain my master's degree in human resource management.

Work and school kept me very busy and that made the time that my husband was on deployment go by fast, which was great. But the time was here, and it was time for my husband to return home to me from deployment. He was able to return a little earlier than expected and that gave our family from Tennessee time to come out for a visit, which was a good thing because we had not seen them since we left.

I was not feeling well at that time, so I was encouraged to go see my doctor. I had always been a person who was never sick, so this was strange to me that I was feeling ill. After my appointment and the doctor ran a few tests, he informed me that I was about four weeks pregnant. It was unexpected news that my husband and I would now be having our first child. I was so happy and excited, but I was still nervous. My husband didn't go to the appointment with me because he and I both suggested that he didn't need to. Because this was only supposed to be a checkup appointment. Therefore, as soon as I was in my car, I called him and gave him the fantastic news. We decided that we would wait till my second trimester to inform our friends and family of this wonderful news because we wanted to ensure that the baby was fine and I did not have a miscarriage. In the meantime, there was a new person to report to the command I was currently at. Stanita at that time was a single mother of three small children. She and I developed a good work relationship that would soon progress into more.

The time had come for my husband and me to revisit the doctor to find out the gender of the baby. I scheduled an appointment around both of our work schedules so that we both could attend. I was praying for a boy, and my husband was praying for a girl. The doctor conducted the fetal ultrasound (sonogram), which is an imaging system that uses sound waves to produce images of a baby and we all could clearly see what the gender of the baby was. Once the doctor confirmed the ultrasound, he announced that we were having a baby boy. My husband jumped for joy and was so thrilled, and I was so overjoyed. After getting settled in the car, we decided to call our family and let them know the fantastic news. Then soon after, we went out to celebrate. We chose to celebrate because we were so excited that we were about to have a baby. We called our parents first, Edward called on his cell phone, and I called on mine.

Chapter 3

NAVY LIFE, NAVY WIFE

Stanita and I developed a great working relationship, which developed into something a little more. Since I was pregnant and my husband was deployed, my activities at work, school, and church were now my life as there was not much else for me to do.

I was now six and a half months pregnant and taking my second to last college class, and my husband was on a six-month deployment. I awoke in the middle of the night alone with a pain in my stomach. I rubbed my stomach and talked to my baby telling him that everything was okay. After that, I said a prayer to myself and tried to go back to sleep. At that time, I didn't think that I was in labor because it was too soon, and my husband was on deployment and his ship was in the middle of the ocean. That night I could not sleep at all; I tossed and turned all night with the movements of my baby boy and the pain that I endured, and yet, I still did not think I was in labor.

The next morning, I was up bright and early, dressed and ready for work, and still in pain. I still didn't think I was in labor and I just wanted to go to work and have a normal day. But soon, I found out that this particular day would forever change my life. Once I arrived to work and made it to my desk, my coworkers began to arrive and I was in even more pain now than before. Stanita arrived and we both said our good morning greeting, but she looked and asked if I was okay. I said yes, and she went to her desk. With me not able to do much while sitting at my desk, I stumbled over to where Stanita was sitting. Then I stood at her desk with my hand on my stomach and asked her, "Could you do me a favor?"

She said, "Sure!"

"Could you take me to the hospital?" I asked. Without hesitation, she got her things and loaded me in her car, and we were off to Balboa Naval Medical Center, San Diego.

Once we arrived at the hospital, Stanita found me a wheelchair to rest in because I was in so much pain that I could not walk. We proceeded to labor and delivery as recommended by the staff at the medical center. It felt like a lifetime had passed before we located labor and delivery. When we arrived, Stanita explained my symptoms to the nurse and she checked my stomach and informed me that I was in labor! This couldn't be true. I said to that same nurse, "It's too early for me to deliver. My baby is not due for another two months." But the nurse reassured me that everything would be okay and that the baby did not have any more room in my stomach, and he was ready.

The nurses got me set up in a room, and I changed into a hospital gown. After that, they hooked me up to a machine. The first thing I heard was my baby boy's heart beating strong and fast, and it was the best sound at that moment because that assured me that I was going to be a mommy soon.

While lying there, Stanita began to make phone calls to my family and friends letting them know that I was in the hospital in labor. She then emailed my husband and told him what had happened. The time was here for me to begin to *push* because my son was coming whether I wanted him to or not. As I began to push, Stanita was right by my side assisting me in what the nurses requested from me. After a few more instructions to push, we heard a cry, and he was finally here. Ethan Zachary was born at 1:11 p.m. He weighed four pounds twenty-two ounces and was nineteen inches long.

The nurse allowed me to hold and talk to him. I loved him and welcomed him into my life. But soon, the nurses informed me that they would have to take him to the Neonatal Intensive Care Unit (NICU) to help him develop a little more. Stanita informed me that she spoke with my mother and she would be in town the next day. For the time being, Stanita and a few of my other friends stayed right by my side.

As we awaited, the nurses had to move me from labor and delivery to another room. I looked at Stanita and said, "Thank you." Then I said, "Hey, godmomma, you're stuck with us for life now." She looked at me strangely, and I said again, "You are stuck with us. Welcome to being Ethan's godmother."

I was then diagnosed with preeclampsia symptoms and HELLP syndrome (hemolysis, elevated liver enzymes, low platelet count); that's what caused me to go into labor weeks before I was actually due.

Ethan was now one week old and still in the NICU, and I had been released from the hospital. At that time, Edward was granted permission to return home to see Ethan and me. When I picked him up from the airport, we went straight to the hospital so that he could see his son. For the next twenty-one days, Ethan remained in the NICU, getting better and stronger each day. My husband and I were at the hospital day and night visiting Ethan, talking and praying for him. After twenty-one days in the hospital, we were granted permission to take him home, and boy, we were grateful and excited. Once Ethan was released, Stanita came by our home while I was on maternity leave to see Ethan. She even brought her kids to meet him as well.

Stanita and I have become really close since the birth of my son. She came over to visit her godchild (that's what she calls him). It was good to see her every time she would come over. She would always come over bringing him gifts that he did not need. She would often bring her kids over so they could see their new little brother. I even established an excellent relationship with her kids as well. My relationship with Stanita has developed into a delightful friendship, and that really helped me because my husband had to return to complete his deployment.

The time had come for me to return from my maternity leave after a total of sixty-eight days at home with my son. I was not ready to leave my baby, but I was blessed to have a stay-at-home nanny that would come to our house and stay until I get off at work. Thus, I didn't have to get my baby up and out of the house, which was a complete blessing. I was still on active duty at this time, so it was a blessing that I did not have to take him outside of the house for the first year of his life.

After being at work for a few months, I reached the end of my military obligation. I would have to either reenlist or officially separate from the navy. After discussing it with my husband, we decided that I would separate from the US Navy after eleven years of service. This was a bitter yet sweet decision. For me, it was something I needed to do after my service on two ships, being stationed in Italy and Japan, meeting my amazing husband, obtaining three degrees, and meeting some of the most incredible friends and family while in the navy. It was now time to focus on being a wife and mother and supporting my husband as he pursued his naval career.

Chapter 4

WHERE DID THE TIME GO?

April 2013

Four years have come and gone, and the time has come for me and my husband—and now my son—to depart San Diego, due to my husband being reassigned back to Tennessee. We've truly had a pleasant stay in San Diego. We've met some magnificent people along this journey, and we will forever have a bond with them. The memories that were produced in San Diego will never be forgotten.

I decided that I wanted to try and return to the navy on active duty, so I made a medical appointment the Friday before we were due to leave the area. The appointment consisted of blood work, magnetic resonance imaging scan (MRI), computed tomography scan (CT scan), and a physical test to see if I was clear to return to active duty. After the doctors received the test results and reviewed them with me, they informed me and my husband that they saw a tumor, the size of a football, on my left kidney. The doctor gave me only six months to live if I didn't have nephrectomy. Mind you, I had no idea that anything was wrong with me. I felt I was the "picture of health."

I never had to take any medication, and I tried to stay physically fit. I had no related symptoms to show that I had a tumor of that size on my kidney. The doctors would not let me leave the hospital; therefore, I called my husband, and he called our family and friends to inform them of the prognoses and let them know that I was scheduled for surgery first thing that following Monday morning. With this news, family and close friends that lived in the San Diego area stepped in and took care of my then two-year-old son, and my husband called Stanita who was then stationed in Northern California. He called Stanita just to let her know that we had not left the area and told her about the prognoses from the doctors.

I spent the weekend in the hospital with my husband right by my side, questioning God. I kept thinking, *Why me? Why do I have a tumor on my kidney? How did I develop this tumor on my kidney, and what could I have done differently to avoid this?* I was blaming myself for not eating correctly and not drinking enough water. There was so much that was going through my mind at that time, not knowing that this was all a part of God's divine plan for me and my life. Stanita, her male friend (her soon-to-be husband), and the kids came to visit me before surgery and see Ethan for the weekend.

My mother-in-law and sister-in-law came to see me, and they took my Ethan back with them so that my husband and I could focus on me getting better and getting released from the hospital. On April 1, Monday, at 7:30 a.m., I went into surgery to have my left kidney removed. Not knowing what to expect after surgery, I was nervous and afraid. I did not know how I would live without my left kidney. But the doctors assured me that I could live a long healthy life with just one kidney. My husband and I said a quick prayer before the surgery, and off I went.

I was told the surgery took five hours, but it was a huge success. My husband and I were so relieved because it was my first surgery and I did not know how it would turn out. I stayed in the hospital for five days after the surgery and then I was released. I was directed to remain in the area of San Diego so that I could attend a follow-up appointment within a week. After that one week, my doctor approved me to travel so I could leave San Diego and head to Tennessee. The doctor that performed my surgery recommended that I should find a nephrologist in the greater Memphis area or surrounding areas. Since I had only one kidney, my doctor recommended that the nephrologist should monitor my right kidney for any signs of issues, including tumor growth.

Once I returned to Tennessee, I did not find a nephrologist right away because I did not feel it was important to me. I felt good, and I felt that I would be okay and did not want to go to any more doctors. The doctors told me I could live a healthy life with one kidney and that was good enough for me. My husband constantly encouraged me to locate a nephrologist so that I could have my right kidney examined, but I was against it and did not feel that it was necessary. So many times we think we know what's best for us, we think that praying to God will be enough and that we do not need to seek professional medical attention, but that is not true. God placed doctors and nurses in those positions to assist those who may need the assistance. We have to be wise and take the help when it is there for us. After few months, I finally did a little research and soon found a nephrologist. I made an appointment, and he ran tests and had x-rays taken of my right kidney. And all was well...or so I thought.

Chapter 5

HEALTH CHECK

We were so happy to be back in Tennessee and be close to family and friends again. Stanita and I continued to text, FaceTime, and call to check in with each other from time to time. Also, my new nephrologist was a great doctor. He had me set for monthly appointments to check my right kidney. During one appointment, he recommended that I schedule an evaluation with Vanderbilt Medical Center in Nashville, Tennessee, to attempt to get on the list for a kidney transplant. Not sensing anything was wrong, my nephrologist wanted me to go through the process and attempted to get me a kidney.

I made the arrangements and set up an appointment for my husband and me. While going through a process such as this, it is very important that the person you can trust and depend on will attend the appointments with you so that you are not alone. My husband and I left my son with family, and we took a three-hour road trip to Nashville to attend a few appointments and my kidney evaluation. We sat through the educational class for kidney transplants which was a three-hour session. Afterward, we sat with the doctors and nurses as they reviewed my pathology report—a report that gives a cause and effect of disease and/or injury.

Once they reviewed all of the documents including the labs taken, they brought me and my husband into one of the offices to discuss the results with us—if I was approved to be on the list for a new kidney. They broke the news—which also broke my heart. I was not approved to be placed on the list because it had been less than five years since my tumor was removed. Medical regulations state that if a person has a benign tumor within a five-year window of evaluation, that person is not or cannot be approved for a kidney transplant.

When the doctors delivered the news, I collected my things and thanked them for their time. Then my husband and I exited the building and headed home. The minute I got in the car, I broke down and began to cry, asking God, *Why me? Why can't you bless me with another kidney? I am your child, God.* I also began to regret going to the nephrologist in the first place because then I would not have

received this terrible news from the doctors in Nashville. As I continued to cry, my husband just let me. He caressed my back and let me
cry at that moment. After I was done crying, my husband began to
minister to me in the most loving and sweetest way. He simply told
me that everything happens for a reason and in due time and due
season, God would bless me with a kidney. He continued to tell me
to keep praying, trusting, and believing that God will bless me with
a new kidney. He then told me to keep living with the one kidney I
had until my prayers were answered in God's time because I could
live a normal and healthy life with one kidney.

After that day, my life was not the same. I began to read the Bible
more and meditate with God's word daily. I began to have monthly
appointments, which included laboratories with my nephrologist,
and he continued to check my right kidney function by looking at
my creatinine levels/percentage. This helps the nephrologist screen
my kidney for disease, diabetes, high blood pressure, or other con-
ditions that increase the risk of kidney disease. My nephrologist has
discovered that I now had a kidney disease affecting my right—and
only remaining—kidney. Within those monthly appointments and
labs and medical evaluations, he found a few little spots on my right
kidney and recommended that I see a urologist. I was so against

going to see another doctor because of my past experiences. But it was highly recommended because the nephrologist wanted me to have a second opinion on the spots he had seen; he thought they could be cancerous.

I made my appointment with a urologist, and he ran more tests so that he could make an assessment. He discovered that those spots on my right kidney were renal cell carcinoma (RCC), which is a slow-moving cancer. In my case, it had progressed to stage three at that time. The urologist didn't want to proceed with surgery at that time, but he wanted to keep an eye on it to see if the cancer would progress and/or the spots would get smaller. Of course, I was praying the cancerous cells would shrink.

Stanita called to check in with us and, of course, to talk to her godchild. She was now stationed in Louisiana (on shore duty), which was about six hours away from where we live. I told her everything that was going on with me and what prognostic was with my kidney. Even with all that, I reassured her that I was totally fine and I would be fine. At that point in my life, I was determined to live my life the best way I knew how and to be there for my husband and my son even though I still didn't know what was to come.

Chapter 6

HARSH REALITY

I discovered in my monthly appointments with my nephrologist that my kidney function continued to decline, but I didn't feel as though I was "ill" and needed to take it "easy." I also didn't tell many people that I had kidney disease because I didn't want them to worry about me, and I did not want people to look at me as if I was not a regular person. Sometimes, when we let "the world" know what we "have" or what we are dealing with, they seem to look at you differently or look down on you. I felt it was something that my husband and I would pray about and deal with together. My right kidney at that time was functioning at about 30 percent and was failing by the day it seemed. I was beginning to feel more fatigued than normal. I felt tired, drowsy, and I had no energy to do most things that I normally would, but I thought it was just because I needed more sleep at night.

One night in January 2017, my husband and I were finishing up dinner with our son, and I stepped away and went to our bedroom for a minute to grab something. Ethan decided to follow me to our bedroom, and I said to him, "Go back to Daddy. I'm okay. I don't need you to follow me." But he refused and still wanted to follow me, and I let him. The next thing I knew, I was getting up from the floor because I had just had a seizure and my then five-year-old son was there the entire time I was seizing. My husband told me that Ethan yelled his name and told him to come into the bedroom. Once my husband arrived, he saw me on the floor shaking uncontrollably and he immediately called 911.

Once I awoke from the seizure and the emergency response team was en route to our home, I looked over at my son and I could see the terror in his eyes. I felt so bad for him at that moment, and there was nothing I could do for him. But I heard my husband coaching him through, telling him not to cry, and to be a "big boy" for Mommy. By the time the emergency response team arrived at our home, I was alert knew where I was but just didn't know what happened. The team asked me if I wanted to ride in the ambulance with them or ride with my husband in our car instead. I told them that my husband would take me because I wanted to ensure that Ethan was taken care of first.

I changed my clothes. My husband called my best friend to come and get Ethan, and we went straight to the emergency room (ER) in one of the local hospitals. As any ER at 11:00 p.m., it was completely busy and full of people seeking medical assistance, so I checked myself in at the front desk and waited to be seen. As my husband and I were sitting in the waiting area, I was feeling fine as if nothing happened, and we began to laugh and talk. But suddenly, I passed out while waiting to be called. When I awoke, I had oxygen on my face and was in a back room. The nurses were asking me questions, and I saw my husband looking a little apprehensive, which concerned me because I didn't know what happened. The nurses informed me that I had just had another seizure in the ER waiting room.

Finally, I was placed in a hospital room for the night, and the next day, the doctors made their rounds. They would be in to check on me and give my husband and me the results from the test that they ran the previous night. My husband left me that night and went to check on Ethan and returned just in time for the doctor to give us the results. I was assigned a neurologist, and he informed us that I had seizures the night before because my kidney was failing. The neurologist advised us that I would be able to go home, and prescribed me seizure medication to control the seizures—Levetiracetam, also known to many as Keppra. Keppra may also cause drowsiness and affect your ability to drive or operate machinery. As the doctor was telling me that last little bit of information, I felt as though the air had been lifted from my body. I could not drive for at least six months. The doctor stated that we would revisit the issue in six months to how I was doing and if I had any seizures during that time.

I felt like I was once again being punished for something, and I was back asking God, *Why me? I'm already in kidney failure, and now I am taking medication that affects my ability to drive. And on top of that, I will be dependent on my husband and family to get me around?* I was devastated and heartbroken, and I felt as though God was not hearing my silent prayers.

As always, Stanita called to check in with us and talked to her godchild. I informed her of my seizure and hospital stay. Then I opened up to her about my kidney failure. She was very encouraging and asked what she could do for us. I just informed her that there was nothing she could do but pray for me and my family. Grateful to go back to working full days but still not driving, God blessed me with a great coworker who lived near me and volunteered to pick me up every morning and drop me off at home for the next six months. During that difficult time, my magnificent husband continued to take care of me and our son while I was down.

Chapter 7

LORD, HEAR MY PRAYER

As I tried to live my life as best as I possibly could, my right kidney was still failing. During one of my many appointments with my nephrologist, he informed me that I had stage four kidney cancer and I needed to start hemodialysis immediately. At first, I was against it because I was trusting God to bring me through this ordeal. Every time I would meet with my nephrologist, he would discuss dialysis, but he would never move forward with it because I was never displaying any symptoms of RCC or a kidney disease. I knew that God was helping me get through this stormy season in my life.

I had yet another appointment, but this one was with my urologist. He ran more tests, and the spots that were on my right kidney had grown larger. The urologist was concerned that the cancer would spread, so he scheduled me in for a biopsy (an examination of tissue removed from a living body to discover the presence, cause, or extent of a disease) to check the growth on my kidney. Once I completed the biopsy, I met with my urologist a week later and we reviewed the results. He recommended surgery to have part of my kidney removed and to see a general surgeon to discuss the option.

I was happy to hear this news. Removing part of my kidney meant I didn't need a kidney transplant, and I did not have to go on dialysis and get back to "normal" or so I thought. My husband and I went to see the general surgeon at a local hospital to discuss if I could have a portion of my remaining kidney removed. The surgeon was totally against removing part of my kidney because in my case, the remaining portion would not be enough for my kidney to still function normally. Therefore, the surgeon's recommendation was to remove my only remaining kidney. There was no other option but to follow the doctors' orders, and we scheduled surgery instantly because the spots were not getting smaller and he did not want the cancer to spread. Here I am finding myself asking my famous question, *Why me? Don't you think I've been through enough?*

My nephrologist wanted me to have my first dialysis treatment before my surgery. Before my right nephrectomy, I had to have an outpatient procedure done and get an arteriovenous (AV) fistula inserted in my left upper arm as well as a venous catheter inserted in my upper right chest area. An AV fistula is a connection that's made between an artery and a vein for dialysis access. This surgical procedure is completed by stitching together two vessels to create an AV fistula. A central venous catheter is a plastic tube placed in a large central vein in the neck. Catheters are tunneled; they go under the skin of the chest and into a vein in the neck. I needed these two devices at that time because the venous catheter was something I could use imminently for dialysis, and the AV fistula needed time to "develop" or "mature." An AV fistula frequently requires two to three months to develop or mature before the patient can use it for hemodialysis. The procedure took about three hours, and then I was sent home to rest and recover before my first treatment.

Chapter 8

LIFE ON DIALYSIS

Hemodialysis is a procedure where a dialysis machine and a special filter, called a dialyzer, are used to clean your blood. The machine removes waste-like product in the form of liquid from a person's body. So that was it. There I was, a thirty-seven-year-old dialysis patient. I have prayed to God asking him to help me to get better, help me not to have to take dialysis because I feel fine. I lived an active life; I felt dialysis would only slow me down. I would not be able to live a "full" life as I wanted to. I felt like I was above dialysis; I felt dialysis was for "sick" people, and I was not sick. I felt it would prevent me from traveling as I *loved* to do.

My husband and I arrived at the clinic early to sit and observe. Patients came in, sat, and waited with us; and some left when their treatment was over. The patients were of all different age groups;

some were older than me, and some were younger. Then my name was called, and it was my turn to go to the back and get my first treatment. I was so nervous. My husband asked the nurse what time he should return to pick me up, and they informed him that I would be finished in three hours.

I went to the back, the nurses asked me to remove my shoes and step on the weighing scale while they recorded my weight for my patient file. It's important that your dialysis team weighs you at every appointment and keeps track of any changes. Your weight affects how much fluid to remove during dialysis. Your doctor and nurses will determine your dialysis estimated dry weight without extra fluid. The nurse directed me where to sit, and as I took my seat, I looked around and saw two rows of chairs that looked like reclining chairs at a hospital. Next to each chair was a machine. Some of the patients in the dialysis room were sleeping, some were reading, some were up talking to each other, and others were taking snacks.

The nurses introduced themselves and explained to me what was about to take place. The nurse's responsibilities include checking the patients' vital signs, talking with them to assess their condition, teaching patients about their disease and its treatment, and answering any questions. The nurses oversee the dialysis treatment from start to finish. I signed some paperwork that gave the clinic permission to care for me. And after that, the nurses covered my chest, put on their gloves, cleaned the area where the venous catheter was located with alcohol wipes, pulled my venous catheter out, and then connected me to the machine to my catheter and my three hours began.

I sat there on the machine with my eyes closed still questioning God, thinking, *Why me? Why am I here, God? Why am I on dialysis? I should be at work right now, God. I could be doing so many other things, God.* I was angry, and I wanted to be in any other place than in that room. And it's like I heard a small still voice say, *Why not you?*

At that moment my life changed for the better. It's like God was telling me, *Why not you? You are no better than the next person.* After the three-hour treatment, I made up my mind that I would have a better attitude about dialysis. I wanted to do more than just complain about something I could not change. I wanted to start thanking God for dialysis. I began to call this time in my life, "my season of dialysis." Seasons change, and I sincerely believed that soon, this season in my life would come to an end. I must endure this season and stay my course in which God has laid before me (Psalm 119). I began to start journaling about my season of dialysis, and that time spent, writing really helped me through. Dialysis had really given me time to connect with myself, to evaluate those things that are most important to me.

From that day on, three days a week for three hours of my life, I would be receiving dialysis treatment, and I began to look at this in a positive light. God provided me with a way to continue to live and be there for my family. From that day on, I never questioned God as to why I continued to pray for a kidney transplant. Whether I received a living donor kidney or one from a deceased donor, I just knew that God was going to bless me. But in this new season, I would be grateful that I was alive (1 Corinthians 10:13).

As always, Stanita and I were communicating to check in on one another talked to her godchild, Ethan. She asked how I was, and I told her the current situation. It always seemed like whenever we spoke, my situation has changed from the last call. Even though we sent text messages many times in between, I never told her what was really going on. I never wanted anyone to worry about me. So I explained my situation and when I was having surgery, as she was very unfamiliar with the process. She said she would try and come to Tennessee the day of my surgery, and I insisted that she did not because I was going to be fine.

October 25, 2017, the day finally arrived for my second surgery to remove my remaining kidney. Again, I was nervous, but I prayed that God's will be done and that all would be well. I thought to myself, *I won't have any kidneys. I don't know of a person that doesn't have any kidneys.* On the day of the surgery, I had a huge group of family and friends there to support me. We all said a prayer, and the time came for the nurse to wheel me back to surgery.

After a successful three-hour surgery, my husband and I were in my room and we met with the surgeons who performed my surgery. They explained everything that happened and discussed the next steps. They explained that since I didn't have any more kidneys, I would not produce any urine, which was totally new for me. Also, I was placed on a strict low sodium diet, and my fluid intake was limited to thirty-two fluid ounces a day, which is not much because that number includes your meal as well as the liquids consumed within a day.

When I heard this news, I thought to myself, *With no kidney, how will I flush the liquids from my body in between dialysis treatments?* I was very nervous, but I had to trust this process and have faith that God's will be done. My mom was with me every day while I was in the hospital, and Edward was able to work and take care of Ethan.

While I was in the hospital, the nurses would come every other day to take me to the dialysis center in the hospital for three hours a day. On the fifth day in the hospital, the doctors released me and let me go home. I was happy to be going home, but I was nervous about what was yet to come.

Once released to go home, Stanita called my husband and checked on me and asked if we needed anything. When she spoke with me, she asked me what the process was for her to be tested so that she could donate a kidney. I was against that thought because I did not feel that she should go through major surgery for me. I turned down her request, and we moved on. Every day I was at dialysis faithfully getting my treatment and still living life as normally as I possibly could. Dialysis for me was great. It made me feel better. It gave me that "boost" of energy that I needed every other day. When I was living with my right kidney function at less than 10 percent, I was very sluggish and tired, but I didn't know that my kidney function was the reason. Thus, I was able to still work full time.

I would go to dialysis at 5:00 a.m., sit through my three-hour treatment, and then go to work. I was so blessed to work with a fantastic team that knew my situation and supported me through it. I was still able to take a vacation with my family and friends.

This season of dialysis really increased my faith as well as my prayer life. I grew so much closer to God. Yet, amid that difficult season, I had a wonderful pastor and first lady along with my church family who continued to pray for me and with me, and that support really encouraged and blessed me during that time.

God knew exactly what he was doing when he sent me through this struggle. My church family had a movie night event with the movie *A Question of Faith*, which tells the moving story of a pastor whose faith is put to the test while grappling with the many issues faced by everyday people. One episode in this movie includes a tragedy from texting while driving and the need for an organ and tissue donation. All people from the surrounding area and churches were welcomed to the event, and there was someone from Donate Life America to help people register people to become organ, eye, and tissue donors. I was the speaker for the evening just to share my story.

Even though I did not have any kidneys, I was still under the care of my nephrologist. He suggested that I attend the event to get my name on the United Network for Organ Sharing (UNOS) list so that I could possibly get a kidney soon. It had been five years since my first nephrectomy surgery and I was eligible to start the process. He recommended that I begin to talk with friends and family members to see if they would like to get tested to donate a kidney to me. I began to talk to a lot of my family members only because I did not feel as though any of my friends would want to donate. Through this process, Stanita and I spoke more and more because she would call or text to check in on me. She and I began to talk and again told me that she wanted to get tested to see if she could donate. I was still against her donating, though I am not sure why, but I just did not want her to go out of her way to do this for me. I just didn't feel that I was deserving.

Stanita was not a blood relative, so I did not want to put her through anything like that. She simply stated, "I have two kidneys and you can have one."

I then asked her, "What about your children? What if they needed a kidney?"

She said, "Between the three of them, they have six kidneys. They'll be okay." She and I went back and forth via phone calls about her donating, and I then asked her to speak with her husband.

When he and I spoke, he told me, "You know, once she puts her mind to want to do something, there's no way of stopping her." I asked for his blessing, and he said he supported whatever she wanted to do. Plus, if it was going to keep me alive longer, then he was all for it. I asked her if I could think about it, and she agreed. My husband and I prayed about it, and he encouraged me to allow Stanita to be tested. The worst thing was that she was not a match. So we both agreed to go forward with the process, but we came to a bump in the road. I was not on any list with UNOS, and that was a problem.

I then went back to my nephrologist informing him that I had a few people that wanted to get tested to donate a kidney, and he then gave me a list of three hospitals within Memphis and the surrounding areas. One was the University of Mississippi Medical Center in Grenada, Mississippi (UMMC), one hour and thirty minutes south of Memphis; the next was Vanderbilt in Nashville, Tennessee, three hours east of Memphis; and the last was Methodist University in Memphis, Tennessee. I had been to Vanderbilt back in 2014 when I was first denied being placed on the UNOS list, and I had to go back through the process all over again.

Chapter 9

FOLLOWING THE PROCESS

It's been five years since my first left nephrectomy, and I was approved to begin my evaluation process in hopes that I would be able to get a living donation from Stanita or a deceased donation from someone else. My first appointment to begin the approval process to be placed on the list with UNOS was at UMMC Grenada. My husband and I set the right time that the both of us could get off at work so we could attend the education class, labs, and the doctor's visit, which is a requirement. We were able to take Ethan to Edward's Parents so that he and I could attend the appointment at UMMC Grenada. Those appointments took a day for us to complete, and then we headed back home. After that, I waited for the phone call from UMMC Grenada with the approval that I was now on the list.

During this time, I was still going to dialysis treatment three days a week for three hours a day; going to work after dialysis, and then also taking care of my family at home. Within the waiting time, the staff at Vanderbilt contacted me to set up an appointment to complete the evaluation just as I did with UMMC. In September, while waiting for time to pass to attend my appointment in Nashville, UMMC Grenada called me with some wonderful news of me being approved to be placed on the UNOS list in Mississippi.

Imminently, I began to give God all the praises because I had been on dialysis for less than a year, and I was already approved to be on the UNOS list. What that meant was, if there's a kidney available that matches my blood type, then UMMC would contact me and I would have to drive to Jackson, Mississippi, for the kidney transplant surgery. My Vanderbilt appointment was at the end of September, and of course, it was the same process that I completed while at UMMC.

October had finally arrived (my birthday month), and it was also my dialysis anniversary—meaning that I had been on dialysis for one year by this point. During that year, I struggled emotionally and physically not knowing when God would bless me with a kidney. I was not feeling my best, but I continued to press on and do what I was supposed to do within this season of my life. I did not give up or give in; I kept pressing on and kept trusting in God's promises. My birthday had come and gone. I received a call from an anonymous number, and I almost did not answer it. But I am glad I took the call as it was Vanderbilt calling me with some great news. I had been approved to be placed on the UNOS list with Vanderbilt. What an amazing birthday gift to receive.

I then gave all my potential living donors the information for both the hospitals so that they could contact them and get the evaluation process started. It was not encouraged that I take part in the process for the living donors' evaluations because they may not be a match and/or they may change their minds about donating. Not knowing where any of my living donors were with their evaluations, I continued to attend my early morning treatments at the dialysis clinic and continued to go to work after the treatments. A few days later, I received a call from Stanita. I answered just thinking it was one of her "check-in" calls, but I heard her yelling something that I could not understand. So, I asked her to calm down and speak slowly.

She yelled, "I'm a match!" I thought it was all a dream, *She can't be serious, can she*? So I began to ask questions and began to cry all at the same time.

The Nurse at Vanderbilt called and told her that she was a perfect match, and it was as if we were blood relatives because our blood matched so well. I began to reminisce about her and me meeting years ago in San Diego, not knowing then that we met for a special reason—and this was that reason. God had our paths cross back then because he knew that I would need a kidney and she would be a match. He knew that she would be not just a match but a perfect match for my kidney transplant surgery (to God be the glory). There are wonderful benefits for patients who can receive a kidney from a live donor. The recipient of a living donor kidney usually lives a longer healthier life compared to those who receive a kidney from a deceased donor. Personally, I would have taken a deceased kidney and/or living kidney, but I'm grateful God blessed me with a living donor kidney. I know in my heart that this entire situation was all a part of God's perfect plan (Jeremiah 29:11).

For the next steps, we had to set up a date for Stanita to go to Vanderbilt to start the evaluation process so we could move forward with the transplant surgery. Keep in mind, Stanita is still on active duty, a wife and a mother, so Vanderbilt had to work with her around her schedule. While we were waiting to complete this process, I was called by Methodist University Hospital in Memphis, Tennessee, to come and began my evaluation with them just as I had done with UMMC Grenada and Vanderbilt in Nashville, Tennessee. My husband and I scheduled a date and time for this evaluation, and we went in for a day of that. This evaluation was like the others; and after I completed the education class, labs, and spoke with the doctors and nurses, I received a call that same week with approval that I had been placed on the list there at Methodist University Hospital.

Now it was up to me to decide where I wanted to have my kidney transplant surgery. Stanita had an appointment with Vanderbilt in Nashville in December of that year, but she left it up to me to decide where I wanted to have my surgery. I spoke with my husband, and he left that decision up to me to pick the hospital that I wanted. I chose Methodist University because I felt that it was a better choice for the stability of our then seven-year-old son, and we would have a little help from our family and friends in the area to assist with him as well. After I made that decision, I called Stanita and gave her the nurses' information for Methodist University.

Chapter 10

LIVING DONOR

During the process of any living donor evaluation and discussion, the prospective recipient is not included because the doctors don't want to alarm the recipient in the event the donor is not willing to donate and/or not able to donate. But I continued to pray that everything would work out in my favor and praying that Stanita would be able to donate. Through this process, there were so many people praying for me: my husband, my family, my pastor, my church family, and friends. So there was nothing more for me to do but to continue attending dialysis and continue to stay on the same path I was on. I had to trust the process and trust in God's timing for me and my situation. God's will be done.

Stanita had been approved for a two-day appointment at Methodist University Hospital in mid-December, which consisted of labs, a urine sample, a heart scan, an MRI, a CR scan, and so much more. The night she arrived, we went to dinner, and her family and my family spent the night catching up. I decided that if she was able to donate or not, she was forever a part of my family no matter what. Besides, she was Ethan's god mom. After the two-day evaluation, Stanita was approved to leave the area and head back home. Right before the Christmas holiday approached, I was called by the pre-transplant nurse from the Methodist University Hospital alerting me that Stanita was approved. She was a perfect match to donate, and I would receive her left kidney. To God be the glory!

I spoke with Stanita and we discussed a date. She was still on active duty, therefore, we had to work around her schedule. It was not up to me at that point because I would make the time. The scheduled date was set for three months out. To be perfectly honest, I was a little upset about that date because it meant me waiting a little longer to get a kidney, and that was not what I wanted to do. I was approved, and she was approved. We were a perfect match, and I still had to wait. But I didn't question God this time. I had to recognize that it had all been worked out in God's perfect plan and His timing—not my timing. When anything is done in God's timing, it is always right on time (Psalm 27:14).

Stanita and her husband drove into town on Sunday evening because she must complete some day before tests on Monday. So we agreed to meet up for dinner (this included my husband, my son, and her husband). I believe during dinner we both were a little nervous and anxious, thinking about the surgery on Tuesday morning. On Monday, I completed my last dialysis treatment. I had been on dialysis for seventeen long months. This season of my life was coming to an end, and I was so grateful to God that he allowed me to live to see it.

I began to think back to when I got the prognosis of my first kidney, and I had no idea that I would make it to see this date or have this time.

The day was here that I had been waiting for so long! I woke up at 3:30 a.m. because I had to be at Methodist University Hospital at 5:00 a.m. My husband and I felt it was necessary to include my then eight-year-old son in the surgery date because he had been through so much with me.

My family and I were the first ones to arrive at the hospital that morning, and then Stanita and her husband came shortly after. After that, my two good friends, Stanita's father and the first lady of our church, had arrived. Soon, we were all checked in and directed on where to go within the hospital and had to check in there. The nurses assigned us to separate rooms, and we stopped and gathered for a word of prayer for God's healing and protection during the surgery.

Stanita was the first to be taken back for the surgery because the doctors needed to evaluate her left kidney to ensure that the previously ran tests were still accurate. I had to wait about three hours until the nurses came and got me and prepped me for surgery. As they prepared me, I was feeling so excited that the time had come. My husband and I left my friends in the waiting room and went to the next area to wait. To ease my nerves, my husband led us in another prayer. We prayed to God to "ease" the stress of this surgery and asked Him to go into the operating room and touch and be with each and every doctor in the operating room. Then the nurse came and got me for surgery.

Chapter 11

OVERFLOW

Once I awoke from the surgery and was taken to my room, more of my family and friends had arrived. I was completely thrilled to see so many people there in my room and so happy for the support from my family and friends through this process. The medical staff informed me that my surgery took between two to three hours and it went extremely well. The first thing I wanted to know was if the new kidney functioning and producing urine because I stopped producing urine when I lost my last remaining kidney. No one could answer that question but the surgeons, so I waited patiently for the surgeon to arrive to brief me on the surgery.

Once they arrived, I was given the news that the surgery went better than expected; and as soon as the kidney was placed in my body and connected, it began to produce urine. My new kidney produced so much urine that it began to overflow. I instantly began to cry and praise God for this blessing that the kidney was functioning well. Once the surgeons left my room and a few of my guests departed as well, Stanita and her husband came into my room.

Stanita said, "Hey girl." Yes, Stanita was just out of surgery and she was already walking. I broke down once again and cried because I just was so happy to see her doing well and to think about her doing this selfless act of giving me one of her kidneys. It was such a joyous moment.

The next morning, I was up early and out of my bed walking around my room feeling great. I was a little sore, but overall, I felt good. Doctors came in for my morning report/update, and they told me that my new kidney was functioning at 100 percent as if it were my very own. "To God be the glory" is all that I was able to say at that moment. I was only healed because the good Lord set the entire plan in motion. It was totally a "God thing."

The local Memphis news station contacted my husband wanting to conduct an interview with me and Stanita on the process, and we both agreed. Later that day, someone was sent to interview me and Stanita in the hospital on how we met. The news station also wanted to bring awareness and inform people of the importance of being living donors and how one noble act can completely change a person's life. Three days had gone by, and all my tests and bloodwork came back clear, and Stanita and I were granted permission to leave the hospital. Doctors were very shocked and amazed at how well the kidney was responding to my body and how well my body was responding to it. I was not shocked at all because I know what God can do, and he can do anything.

The doctors informed me that I needed to drink a lot of water because water helps the kidneys remove wastes from your blood in the form of urine. Water also helps keep your blood vessels open so that blood can travel freely to your kidneys and deliver essential nutrients to them. Stanita was instructed to stay in the local Memphis area for a full week after being released because she had a follow-up appointment with the surgeons to test that her kidney was functioning at 100 percent. Once I was released, I began to have weekly appointments with a nephrologist at Methodist University to continue to monitor my new kidney.

Usually, when a person receives a kidney transplant (living or deceased), there are antirejection medicines as well as immunosuppressive medicines that they must take for the rest of their lives. I left the hospital that day taking about twenty-six medications a day. One month after the kidney transplant, I had no problems or concerns and my medication was decreased each week I went in to see the nephrologist. I was doing better by the day.

Observed in April each year, National Donate Life Month helps to encourage Americans to register as organ, eye, and tissue donors and to honor those that have saved lives through the gift of donation. I, along with one of the nephrologists, had been asked to speak live at a local Memphis news station about my kidney transplant and donation and also to speak on Donate Life hoping to educate more people. It was important to assist in this cause of raising awareness and increasing the number of organ and tissue donations to help save and heal lives. It is so crucial to foster a culture where organ and tissue donation is embraced as a fundamental human responsibility. That was such an exciting time for me because I never would've thought I would be on television telling my story.

Epilogue

Stanita and I remain sister friends today, and we see each other often. The bond we have is unbreakable, and as I said before, "She's stuck with me and there is nothing she can do about it."

Today, I am continuing to walk in my healing as God orders my steps. My life is going well, and I'm doing great. My kidney is continuing to function at 100 percent, and my doctors are still amazed that I'm doing so well. But as I always have said, this is all a God thing; I had nothing to do with it, and I praise him daily for this.

I had someone asked me, "If you could change one thing about this season in your life, what would it be?"

I answered and said, "I wouldn't change anything for me. I would want to change it for my husband and my son.

Even though this happened to me and my body, it also impacted them as well." Why wouldn't I change anything is because this experience has changed me completely. This season of my life changed my mind and my spirit, and it inspired me to pray more and increased my faith in God.

The first lady of our church spoke once and said, "Seasons come and go. They are not meant to stay the same. Just as there are four seasons, in life, we have seasons, and our seasons are not meant to stay the same. Therefore, embrace the current season you are in, and allow God to work on you." My medical issues with my kidneys only lasted for a time and were only one season in my life. I needed to go through everything that God sent me through to first enhance my faith in him and so that I could be that light to others who may not know God and know what he can do.

Some say that I'm a miracle, but I do not see it that way. I just see myself as a vessel that God has chosen to use. And I would like him to use me to bring awareness to others about living organ donation, and to bring awareness to the world about Jesus Christ.

Acknowledgments

First and foremost, I have to pause and give honor to my Lord and Savior Jesus Christ for without his grace and mercy I would not be here today. Thank you, Lord, for continuing to keep your hand upon me.

To my brother and sister, Larry and Stanita Burton, thank you for your unwavering generosity and your willingness to give of yourself. I am forever grateful to God for connecting us when and how he did.

Stephine Johnson, thank you for the encouragement and giving me the *push* I needed to make this book possible. I appreciate you.

Bayview Baptist Church in San Diego, California, so thankful for everyone at the church who open their hearts to me and my family. I am very appreciative of you all.

Pastor Donald and First Lady Rhonda Johnson and the Oak Grove Missionary Baptist Church Family in Bartlett, Tennessee. I love my church family! Lord God, I thank you for the love and support of this church in my life; God definitely knew what I needed when I needed it, and I am filled with so much gratitude.

Thank you to my beloved family and my friends (you know who you are); thank you for praying for me, praying with me, holding my hand when I did not think I could get through this journey, and thank you for just…showing up!

About the Author

Zainora B. Polk was born and raised in Houston—one of the most populous cities in the state of Texas. She grew up loving Christ and, most importantly, loving her family. She is a wife, mother, and a navy veteran, and considers her faith and family to be most important to her. She loves to travel and try new things. Zainora earned her associate of arts (AA) in general studies in 2006, a bachelor of science (BS) in business management in 2008, and a master of arts (MA) in human resource management in 2011.

The book *Why Me?* is her personal journey of how she got through a very life-changing situation through her faith, family, and friends. Zainora wanted to share this part about her life to encourage someone who is going through a similar situation or just maybe going through a difficult time in life. Ask her and she will always tell you, "Seasons come and go, but remember no two seasons are the same. But if you stand strong and bear your season, you will get through it."

CPSIA information can be obtained
at www.ICGtesting.com
Printed in the USA
LVHW031341200422
716608LV00004B/533

9 781662 468988